I'd Write the Sea Like a Parlour Game

© 2017, Alison Dyer

We gratefully acknowledge the financial support of the Canada Council for the Arts, the Government of Canada through the Canada Book Fund (CBF), and the Government of Newfoundland and Labrador through the Department of Tourism, Culture and Recreation for our publishing program.

All rights reserved. No part of this work covered by the copyrights hereon may be reproduced or used in any form or by any means—graphic, electronic or mechanical—without the prior written permission of the publisher. Any requests for photocopying, recording, taping or information storage and retrieval systems of any part of this book shall be directed in writing to the Canadian Reprography Collective, One Yonge Street, Suite 1900, Toronto, Ontario M5E 1E5.

Printed on acid-free paper
Cover Design Paul Pettipas
Layout by Fenton Fortune

Published by
Killick Press
an imprint of CREATIVE BOOK PUBLISHING
a Transcontinental Inc. associated company
P.O. Box 8660, Stn. A
St. John's, Newfoundland and Labrador A1B 3T7

Printed in Canada by: Marquis

Library and Archives Canada Cataloguing in Publication

Dyer, Alison K. (Alison Kathryn), 1955-, author
I'd write the sea like a parlour game / Alison Dyer.

Poems.
ISBN 978-1-77103-104-2 (softcover)

I. Title. II. Title: I would write the sea like a parlour game.

PS8607.Y356I4 2017 C811'.6 C2016-907458-7

I'd Write the Sea Like a Parlour Game

ALISON DYER

St. John's, Newfoundland and Labrador, 2017

for
my parents
Marion & Don Dyer

Only the most hardy and adaptable can survive in a region so mutable...

Rachel Carson, *The Edge of the Sea* (1955)

Contents

Bones of Paradise

Bones of Paradise | 3
The Foragers | 4
Battle Harbour Triptych | 5
Summer Studies 1 | 7
Summer Studies 2 | 8
Sushi Bar | 9
Irises | 10
Black | 11
Storm | 12
Snowdrops | 13
The Drowning | 14
Hottest Day on Record | 15
The Beckoning | 16
Old Gardens | 17
On Guard for Thee | 18
Transmutation | 19
Erosion: A Sonata in C Major | 20
Awaiting the Perseids | 21
Under the Compass Winds | 22

Apostles of the Boreal

Mountain Ash (the boisterous) | 25
White Birch (the moon child) | 26
Balsam Fir (the trustworthy) | 27
Maple (the flamboyant) | 28
Poplar (the capricious) | 29
Alder (the socialite) | 30
Larch (the erudite) | 31
Juniper (the collector) | 32
White Pine (the white knight) | 33

Apostles of the Boreal (cont'd)

Spruce (the omnipotent) | 34
Pin Cherry (the nursemaid) | 35
Red Pine (the memory stick) | 36

Why He Rested on the Seventh Day

Why He Rested on the Seventh Day | 39
Mind over Matter | 40
Bottled Moose | 41
Ode to the Potato Growers | 42
Hell's Hand | 44
I'd Write the Sea Like a Parlour Game | 45
Ice Flows and Sound Retreats | 46
Nature-deficit Disorder | 47
This Multiplication of Blue | 48

Near Church Street

Capital Haikus | 51
Rock Dove | 52
Chasing Winter Blues | 53
Janubrry | 54
Tattoos of Signal Hill | 55
Wind: excessive | 56
Just Another White-out | 57
Lunch with Alistair | 58
Lament for the Groc & Conf | 59
Evensong | 60
Near Church Street | 61

Acknowledgements

Bones of Paradise

Bones of Paradise

A wild rose spread-eagles my Regal Stove, reposing like a tired flamenco dancer, pink pink against the dirty black metal. A gift from son Ezra who's pulling wheelies on the cove road while daughter Ella, barefoot in skimpy orange shorts, dangles from a damp poplar.

The walk into town is short. Friday evening and the loudest thing is the blaring white of the lighthouse at Custard Head. Save the occasional ATV. Save the off-key clamour of gulls decorating the crab-plant roof.

At Janes' store, over a single purchase, Muriel and I hold a ten minute summit.

The weather.

This morning a biblical rain, spun off another hurricane, has us all thankful we live in Newfoundland.

I wander back to my own craggy piece of paradise in Caplin Cove, wondering how the sun does that here. A bugger of a day and then it throws a bone out over the hillside. Enough to make silver platters of all the puddles. Enough to make the bowl of old meadows shimmer like a litter of kittens. Enough to crescendo the hummocky crest in silent ovation.

The Foragers

A small band scouts the outcrop
like a pack of wild animals
grazing the spine of the hill:
quiet, focused, and shaking off flies.

                                        Later,
with tin and plastic bellies full
they backstretch skyward,
migrate slowly home
licking purple from their fingertips.

Battle Harbour Triptych

Battle Harbour 1

The sea chatting up a storm,
Dentures clacking their white caps.
The spire of ice, yesterday grounded on the shoal behind the church,
is gone. Miles out to sea in search of tourists.

The wind decides to exceed all speed limits.
Ignores the narrow tickle.
Rocks the heavy picnic table outside Tony's house, feigning it might flip it.
Any moment.

Battle Harbour 2

Springy path, scrub willow, rhinestone quartz.
Outcrop with attitude, trip you up if you're not watching.
A world with a view at the top.

Wind playing tag with my camera so my eyes must do the clicking.
Down to the tickle, houses stand straight in their best clothes. Resolute.
Flags salute to the east.

Battle Harbour 3 (Great Caribou Island)

Zigzag up a cliff of lichened rocks and spongy moss,
leaving the cloister of red-white buildings across the slip of blue.
Up down, up down craggy hills,
Sun-dimpled crevices of snow.

Pools of sunset stain the ocean to the west,
Spotlighting islands of rock and blocks of ice.
Inukshuk pointing me home
though a house falls each year.

Summer Studies 1

The children smell of bog water, spruce bark, and wild roses,
pondering equators around planets, fishing questions
                                        Are there allergy eaters in there?
scrambling over brambly land,
naming rocks and pools in the nearby brook,
at night watching slugs mate and
stars shoot.

Summer Studies 2

Secrets revealed:
insides of sea urchins,
beached mermaids' purses,
water strider layovers,
teeth in fox scat.

Lessons learned:
120's by lamplight,
cod jigging with deft fingers,
hens roosting on brown arms,
new monthly blood and missed swims in the brook.

Sushi Bar

Seagulls rage the shore,
aerial whitecaps
scavenge nature's sushi.

Rockweed-wrapped,
egg-gritty,
beach-bar caplin snacks.

Irises

A sea of indigo crests
the cove's green depths. Beyond,

a field of navy waves,
white lips smack the shore. Above

in robin's-egg blue, a caravan of white
prayer flags gather acolytes

bound for the east. And
the blue flags nod, nod.

Black

The only black
and it's skating on thin blue.
Wings extended to keep its balance,
foil gravity.

If I could skate that sky I'd cackle too.

Storm

Thunder rakes in like a Hell's Angels convoy
under a battery of black leather clouds,
fear scattering adults,
trees screeching with kids,
sunset pastels erased, replaced
by sheets of leaden rain
and naked outcrops reach up, shield
against a four-compass-point posse,
galloping across the sky.

Snowdrops

Ephemeral as childhood and running flat out,
a summer garden's memory of winter,
a midnight resolution,
the orientation of a grain of sand,
a cat's preference, or cotton
candy on the back of the tongue.

The Drowning

At dusk, the paper world drowns,
caught in surface tension
with bodies ill-adept for water.

The perfect globe disintegrates,
floats seaward on its Ganges
below a red pyre sky.
In the obsidian ashes of the brook,

it catches a ripple skirting rocks,
with nods from frill-trimmed burnet,
the dying bloom of brookside roses,
the sweet incense of myrica.

Back at the chicken coop, there's a
sawing wail from relatives,
the wasps' memory of home.

Hottest Day on Record

The airwaves drone
with heatwave-sodden fare —
Do you love or hate the heat? Call in.

As platoons of dragonflies
in darning manoeuvres hunt wings
above the cove road, the brook, the fields.

As the hen, in crankiness,
(worms have burrowed deep in parched soil)
takes a dust bath instead.

As bees toil in the thistles,
and ants forage for their queen — drones
and workers getting on with business.

The Beckoning

The woods trail beckons and fungi-hedged,
                — winding through bush and bog —
the boardwalk questions. All shapes
and ages, we answer with castanet steps,

thuds, and mud-caked soles.
Whispers from every shade of green. Nearby,
the shoreline sucks and smacks
with salt on its lips.

Old Gardens

Old gardens are smelled before they're seen.
Thin drifts of lilac
arouse bees in long grasses.

Old gardens draw memories from the ground.
Rippling the earth with forgotten potato drills,
bedded under a strata of sorrel.

Old gardens sigh of long trips to the cellar.
Caved in and cupboards bare, old gardens
ignored of their years of hard labour.

Old gardens are felt before they're seen.
A web of roots, a knot of turf,
worms growing fat, free of prodding steel.

Old gardens do not wait, but
thrive on old compost and new rain,
breed botanical anarchy.

On Guard for Thee

for Roy

Toe positioned in westward stance,
heel toward the eastern trench —
a lone rubber boot, upturned on staff presides
in centre field. A quiet commandant
rallying the troops.

All flanks armoured with bits of fencing,
metal, plastic and noise-making:
a cadre of rusty cans, an infantry of laundry bottles,
an ambush-ready bedspring
in its deep grass position.

Scraps of onion bags, shredded tarps, a regal blue overall,
its arms and legs stuffed and tied with a pink silk scarf,
a cracked orange bucket and —
past kitchen duty but with three good legs left for battle —
a wooden kitchen chair. All enrolled for nocturnal combat.

In Roy's garden, Major Boot,
with a commanding view up the valley,
enlists this band of the crooked, the lost, the rejected
in the twilight war of
vegetables versus moose.

Transmutation

Hauled up from the sea and banked on the garden:
        a weed,
        a wanton dark botany,
        a colour between stop and go?
or a glistening gift of the equinox, now mounded up.

Tresses caressed by caplin and squid,
maybe the occasional orca. A smell like
        a sharp morning of rubbers for striding along the cliff,
        a fog-bound evening wrapped in woolens with sex soon.

Admiring your form: a foreign fur,
deeply rich, entrancing like
        the sheen of late summer bodies
        dancing or fingering a trumpet,
        the colour of porcini mushrooms.

Awaiting your transmutation
        into compost.

Erosion: A Sonata in C Major

Ice

The Isthmus joins the severed limbs of two ancient continents. Or rather one continent — Gondwana — with the oceanic floor of Iapetus. And when it's not shrouded in fog you can see two bays, one on either side of the Isthmus, crowding it with water, testing its rocky limits. The area strewn with erratics, boulders plucked, carried, dropped by retreating glaciers, the erosive force of glacial ice. Now erratics perch on rounded highlands, deep base notes grounding an ethereal landscape.

Waves

From Chance Cove to Western Point the coastline, a symphony in stone. In a quiet sea, kelp gardens below the cliffs sway a lullaby, beach cobbles tap arpeggios, and sea caves belch in timpanic splendour. Narrow sea arches, steep and chiseled, sing arias if tuned in a northwesterly.

Wind

Parabolic, sinuous, curved, blow-out.
        Dry, harsh, parched, draining.
Burgeo Sandbanks, Gooseberry Cove, Windmill Bight. The changing tempo of wind keeps their sand dunes limber, the synergy of granular timbre. These prized spots of erosive excess.

Awaiting the Perseids

A yellow knot of gnats
somewhere before sundown and star bright
irritate the solitary spruce in the cove. Long grass
and all things green melt, pink-gold, down the hillside.

A lone crow caws while gulls, heading home, clutter the sky.
A half-slap of poplar, a slurp of waves play the shoreline —
their echo fizzes off the cliff — and bees jazz up
the fireweed.

Even the rocks, that we scraped across to reach the swimming hole,
tripped over to watch the Perseids perform, yes,
even the rocks soften into toffee: mellow,
at this lonesome, listful end of day.

Then blue turns to white
turns to black
in the bay,
and another day leaves the cove.

Under the Compass Winds

Gulls spindled out of control, jerked up and down like macabre puppets
on invisible strings. The sea had stolen the clouds' silver linings. Jealousy
wasn't green but a cartwheeling wind. The cliffs groaned, shale-shocked,

stuck between the argument, their faces growing darker, furrowed. The row
grew loud. The sea got up on its high horse and spat. The clouds curdled
in disdain. Turned their nimbus backs. And the birds, the barnacles

and tiny crabs — all were caught in the fray. Even the tuckamore,
gridlocked, twisted more, shrunk back. The clouds lashed out.
It started to rain blue black. There was bruising on all sides. We ran

full pelt to the house, slammed the door on them. Stocked
the woodstove and blessed the whistling in the chimney.

Apostles of the Boreal

Mountain Ash (the boisterous)

Uptown you may be the mountain but here
you are the dog.
Berry blues bar for waxwings, starlings
and lost things.
They storm your fruit, splatter your limbs
and stagger away drunk.

White Birch (the moon child)

Some calendar girl you turned out to be.
A barefoot, pale-skinned hippie with the tie-dyed dress
    (*call me Petula or River Song, if you like*).

A real arboreal fashionista.
Not so flashy as the maple (does she or doesn't she?),
no socialist hankerings like the spruce,

but your moon-dappled, tattooed trunk —
    oh so cool —
belies your heat, those BTUs of wild winter love.

Balsam Fir (the trustworthy)

Distinctly dark in June or December,
pine siskin and chickadee will remember,
it's ebony, thick and concealing,
for food, shelter and mates receiving,
pyramidical or tuckamore,
it's dark, dense, and evermore.

Maple (the flamboyant)

For you flip and deal the colour wheel each fall,
        ochre, crimson, purple and persimmon
For locally you are *spicatum* and *rubrum*
For children learn your points, adorn their classroom walls
For you have opposable limbs and a bird's eye for finer things
        and are not jealous of pine for its underfoot warmth
        or of spruce and fir for their hard-earned glow
For you will succeed
For you love the runway, the flight of the debutante's ball
For you anticipate the sweetness of parades, suburban lawns
For you are neither too big nor too small
For you nest in our dreams
For you are honeydew, a sight for sore eyes
For you are hermaphrodite
For you are scarlet, *erable*, *fouereux*, crave the festival
For on your leaves worms curl then spin a circus tent free-fall
For you are ochre, crimson, purple and persimmon
        as you flip and deal the colour wheel each fall.

Poplar (the capricious)

You slap, slap,
like a light rain starting, slither

up in a field of grass,
where you weren't last week, turn

your back to an oncoming storm,
anemic white where green had been, tempt

chickadees, blue jays, the occasional 'pecker —
such an arboreal tease.

Alder (the socialite)

Tracks around the alder's base: desire
lines of two- and four-footed races, with the latest
news printed on glossy pages, those

shrink-wrapped records in early winter snows:
traces of gossip columns, who's in the know;
the obligatory obituary

of who ate who with genuine caution,
a "best places to eat" feature — nibbled
nutlets, bark, and catkins; and ribald

jokes of who peed where; real estate tidbits
on bottomlands, swamps, and roadside ditches;
and the newborn section, with junior's paws

barely scuffing the snow but so like his ma's.
It's all there in print, down around the alders.

Larch (the erudite)

Limber spines at the start of day,
newly baptized in nascent green.

Buds along each branch punctuate:
        "spring arrivals," "wind from the east," and,
            oh yes, the almighty
        "rain, drizzle, and fog."

Each limb a chapter, each tree a book
spreading flamboyant haikus across the barrens:
        ripened
        resplendent
sated.

Monks of the high plateau,
        you go out in flames of ochre,
hover over bogs,
on the periphery of eyes.

And by the pitcher plant
you ditch your pointed grammar.

Juniper (the collector)

No vertical ambition, you assume
a spread-eagle position, accrue granite real estate,
cherish geometric precision. A new design

on growth: horizontal, land-sprawling,
warmth-hugging, wind-shrugging; a prickly complexity,
a basket-weaving approach to maturity. A Kim's Game

with jewels on display: sea-urchin shells, salt-bleached;
jawbones of shrews, doll-sized; ivory skulls of
turrs, porcelain delicate; tooth-studded fox scat;

a warbler's wing with colours like a new musical chord;
and your own blue-chip berries.
Enigmatic in your

sky-cliff existence, stretching seaward
saluting blues
and humpbacks going down.

White Pine (the white knight)

Needles cast to north and bearing compass,
Orion's Belt, in dark of night, your mast —
timbers staged for rough Atlantic crossings,
you sailed, my knight, knew dead men walking.

How many ships were hewn of your fine trunks,
how many men were made to walk your planks?
Such broad shoulders cut a foot or more abreast
squared up to lay men down to rest.

From books and learning, pine-clad hills yet
live in our imagination. Still, I
imagine a tall, straight form unbending
to inclinations of brutal storms, but

for sour merchants quibbling pennies, pounds,
or inches, you, my white knight, stood before
the axe
and fell.

Spruce (the omnipotent)

We are not one. We are the One.

We carpet cliffs against winds; weave
our brothers, entwine our twisted limbs.

We blanket the land: bogs, barrens and outcrops
be damned — or blessed by our verdant fencing.

Our pendulous cones and lichen drapes: aliments
for birds, small mammals, and ungulates.

We shelter both small and large; our quizzical
form for moose, just cunning camouflage.

We recall our past, an ancient group. We grew slow,
advanced upon ice to a kingdom so cool. And now

black or white, we map the north of America, in
union form vast tracts of *glauca* and *mariana*.

For we are not one. We are the One.

Pin Cherry (the nursemaid)

Stand straight.
Red attentions.
Pin up those white aprons.
Join hands together with patience.
Good nurse.

Red Pine (the memory stick)

She's there in plimsoles, gran's hand-knit cardy,
a thin frock carefully ironed, just a little soiled
from an afternoon of den-making in the bracken.

Truth be told I remember you — I hardly remember her at all.
You, sea-green, bottle-brush, upturned
like a teacher's tick in an exercise book,

always backed by blue sky and a sea breeze tasting
like a new flavour of crisps. And dunes nearby.
Holidays.

You were white bread with sandwich spread
and tea in a camp mug. The taste of old plastic.
The family picnic. Sheltering, out of the wind,

leeside of the car in a roadside pull-over. WEL 79.
I recall the license plate. Not the car. Decades later, driving
across this island, that one fine stand of you

overlooking an RV park with patio lights,
horseshoes, wooden cut-out cartoon characters,
and sandy soil. I'd come home.

Why He Rested on the Seventh Day

Why He Rested on the Seventh Day

Roared, erupted, soft and hot.
Spewed viscous pyroclasts.
Hardened into tuff.
Steamed, cooled in showers of thunder.
Strummed, stroked, beaten.
Needled by rain, ice, and salty sea.
Prostrated into pillowed lava.

Mind over matter

Talk to me of gneiss, deep ore
bodies, orogenic belts,
subduction zones,
cross-bedding,
continental drift
as I shift closer,
fall for your fault lines
again.

Bottled Moose

How do you bottle a moose?
she asked, and I knew
with the certainty of an egg
she would keep me happy,
guessing until we were old,
and then some.

Ode to the Potato Growers

May month we'd set potatoes.
Coda Reds, Atlantic Whites, Arran Victories,
Mirton Pearls, May Beauties and nigger toes.
Hauling seaweed to make them grow.

She were born on the date they took seed potatoes out of the cellar.
And skipper goes up and brings her down saying, "I think she'll do for one of my boys."

'Twas seaweed what made our potatoes grow well.
By the tons, come March month or April,
after the ice was over. After ballicater season. And father,
he'd haul a hundred cart loads.

Too much seaweed make your potatoes wet. So wet
that when you eats 'em, there's a wind lopping on your plate.

Set them before going down to Quirpon or the Labrador on a fisherman's ticket.
Do up the ground, a stick down.
Seed potatoes, three across and alley it up,
haul the earth around.

The potato is no thirsty vegetable.
The amount of rain we gets is usually just enough.

Leave the wife to tend the gardens, and the children too —
            if you could walk, you could weed —
between the potatoes, the turnips and
her garden of small seeds.

At night you'd make your bread. Boil an extra potato,
mash it with whatever and make your barm.

Then out of Quirpon or the Labrador come late September or October month.
Start digging them up. Growed forty barrels; 'twere one hundred and eighty pounds to a barrel.
Put them in the cellar pound.

Cow got in the cellar one time and ate the potatoes.
Had some job to get her out, she'd blown up so big.

When spring come 'round, were nothing to put in the pot.
Cabbage was gone, potatoes was gone,
just a bit of salt meat, maybe a dumpling,
'til the next harvest come.

Hell's Hand

Was a sin to dance in the Protestant religion,
and you was going to Hell's fire and brimstone
if you played cards. So we played them
down in the cellar, that our parents wouldn't see
or know what we had in mind.

We'd go out in the night with a milk can,
an old lamp, steal a drop of kerosene.
Burn it with a wick of sheep's wool.
And we'd have a game or two, for an hour no more.
'Twas the warmest place we could find.

I'd Write the Sea Like a Parlour Game

where you scribble a random thought,
fold the paper over. Pass it on. And the
next person adds a line, a truth

or a lie in a few words.
Pressed ink, folded paper, passed along. And so on
'round the table and back to the beginning.

Never the same script.
Never the same story.
Never predictable.

Ice Flows and Sound Retreats
for Jan K

The weight of our mass desires ablates
thick continental glaciers.
Tongues of ice,
eons in silence, speak.

At Christmastime, between
last minute shopping, we share in your journey
from Argentina to Nunavut — your art
installation on ice retreats.

The drip, drip, drip of age-old water belies
the rapid rate of melt. And we drown
in the sound flowing in, out, in, out
on the cusp of Copenhagen.

Nature-deficit Disorder

We stare through the ocean,
blades of rainbows thrash, a Rorschach art,
spawning at the water's edge.

We stare through aquarium glass,
delicate tips and outrageous colours,
wriggling pale tentacles.

That real or robotic? squirms the pink matching Gap.
What would you rather? I ask her,
knowing the answer.

Red-faced, he pounds their bodies into the sand. Play.
I turn and leave these iridescent gifts to rot on the beach
in peace.

This Multiplication of Blue

That impossible fringed purple blue,
a waving wetland of seductiveness,
the annual audience circling Eric's barn.

This year the barn sags still more,
some shingles lost to wild winds,
its west side sinking, the side door ajar.

If you came back today
I'd show you that first,
this multiplication of blue

in spite of everything.

Near Church Street

Capital Haikus

Spring

fog enshrouds
rain penetrates
snow retreats, retreats

Summer

sweet diesel, salt breeze
southside hill ovation
tarmac-warmed buskers

Autumn

armoured skies
free-falling winds
plants on life support

Winter

ice-slicked sidewalks
pedestrians leaning
radio talk shows fire up

Rock Dove

Among soggy butts, wads of gum, and Friday night puke
(barely washed by Saturday's rain) a fine filigree trail,
a fossilized frond, a braille immortalized
in greasy concrete. Rock doves

(not pigeons my daughter reminds) with
feathers like the inside of mussel shells, or
Sunday evenings overlapping cakes and cream
and cerulean skies. Mother chided

the offspring that refused to fly, frustrated
with its clumsiness, then left, rose
upwards with the rest
of her painted throng. Below

the young rock dove stumbled along, nibbling
sidewalk nuisances, and with its clownish gait sank
into heavy cement, not knowing it would make
fine road kill. The shop

next door sells pet paw gel,
a coconut and peppermint salve for earth-bound
cats and dogs.

Chasing Winter Blues

In grayscale November
with sharp thin church spires
and bloated smoke stacks vertical

against the latitudes of crow calls,
pools of slush, and slings of
plastic bags between trees, a noose

flying at Gibbet Hill would seem normal
above the cataract eye of the harbour.

I vow to buy a pair of orange winter boots.

Janubrry

An ice cream scoop of moon
and confetti in the sky
as gulls scratch the night,
hens huddle in the coop.

Ship engines in the harbour drone
and the maples, frozen
in their leafless ineptitude —
unable to drown out the moan.

Months left before heat frees the earth,
warms compost, and worms wriggle
with the hope of spring
and signs of renewal, of birth.

Tattoos of Signal Hill

Knuckles of quartz punched out of bruised purple sandstone,
sea blue with scratch marks from wind and current, and twinkling pools
like barrels of marbles spilt.

A scab of dirty white ice on the chin of George's pond,
and herring gulls, feathering warm and fickle air, spin figure eights
above the hill.

Wind: excessive

Masquerading as ghosts,
a host of unholies
rattles the dresser mirror,

testing soffits, trim, and chimney blocks,
rocking my bed, looking
for that sweet spot of weakness.

Cracking gyproc, creaking frames, and
oh me nerves,
you wind me up.

Just Another White-out

Waking to clapboard flapping,
a skyscape of shifty whites —
(so what if you can't see the bloody harbour)

Humdrum spattering of commuters, arterial bound,
quick-draw scream of police sirens,
Hummers heading to Costco to stock up, lock down.

Neighbours scraping windshield ice,
house-bound dogs barking for escape.
Winter city life, saran-wrapped in ice.

CBC radio staccato *major storm — schools closed; ferries delayed*,
a day explained in sound bites and climatological scales:
        65 centimetres; 50 kilometres; 30 year record.

Another snap-crackle-pop morning.

Lunch with Alistair

I take you to all the best places, I laugh.
Joke about the pen, the dump-cum-engineered landfill,
the funeral home-cum-restaurant.
            I'm in your hands, says the gentle man.

His gait, like his writing process, is slow, measured.
His storytelling, like sweets for good children, metered.
His reading, like a hammock on a boat, rhythmic, lulling.

We talk about this edge of continent, his trip
across the latitudes with polar bears and rifled Inuit guides,
the entire community of La Poile dancing onto the ship

as we munch on a paltry spread of greens
that wouldn't feed my hens —
            How are your hens? he asks —
and I wish we'd ordered the hearty soup,
sustenance for a man full of stories so freely given.

Lament for the Groc & Conf

The old corner stores carried things in ones and twos.
Individual, buy one-at-a-time smokes you needed
to get through the day.

One sold individual aspirins and band-aids
and eggs. Smelled of wet dogs
and mouldy ceilings on dreary spring days.

No muzak blaring. No loyalty points. Just the cadence of missus
behind the counter, bantering about the weather or local politics
with you and Gerry from down the street.

Never more than two customers at a time, unless school was out
and the door set the bell jangling as droopy-jeaned teenagers
ambled in for a quick sugar-salt-fat fix.

Time wasn't wasted looking over a score or more choices of pea soup
or chocolate bars. Two, three brands if you were lucky.
You never bothered checking the expiry date.

Evensong

The vacuum roars on the rug setting, sucking up yesterdays,
exhaling a foul breath. She's looking for god

beneath the sofa cushions, crumbs and dust
disappearing in good orderly direction. Outside,

camouflaging as a maple, a fellow traveller sings to a light rain.
Tulips, slacked-lipped and tired, supplicate. A late spring

baptism. A lone starling builds hope in the neighbour's
rotting clapboard. Seconds later out in search

of promises. Her cat pilgrims to the birdbath, laps
at the rainwater, leaving imprints of its holy

tongue. In a puddle, halos expand, coalesce,
vanish like angels silently popping bubblegum.

Near Church Street
for Marilyn

A late winter afternoon light
illuminates a brigade of trees,
their western halves shining, wizened,
bone white against a fuzzy grey east flank.

Eyes wild, go-go boots, a frail hand
extends. The other clenches
a pink luggage bag on wheels.

She says: Mars lights a new path tonight, and
Do you have a quarter? How about a smoke?
Her silver hair piled high, bare legs crossed,
on duty, near the cenotaph. Another veteran.

Acknowledgements

For creative encouragement, thank you poets and authors David Benson, Mary Dalton, Bruce Johnson, Wade Kearley, and Susan Rendell, among others. Thank you to Michael Crummey, Monica Kidd, and Robin McGrath for reading earlier versions of this manuscript and providing much thoughtful advice.

Thanks to Donna Francis and Pam Dooley at Creative Book Publishing, and to editor Leslie Vryenhoek for her keen eye, light hand and green pen, and book title suggestion.

The following poems (or versions of them) first appeared in these journals. My sincere thanks to the editors: "White Birch (the moon child)" and "Larch (the erudite)" in *Fiddlehead*; "Poplar (the capricious)" in *Grain*; "The Foragers," "Battle Harbour Triptych," "Erosion: A Sonata in C Major," and "Red Pine (the memory stick)" in *The Newfoundland Quarterly*; "Old Gardens" in *Rhythm Poetry Magazine*; "Near Church Street," "Why He Rested on the Seventh Day," "Mountain Ash (the boisterous)," and "Balsam Fir (the trustworthy)" in *Riddle Fence*; and "Evensong" (as "Awaiting the Miracle") in *3 Elements Literary Review*.

The suite of poems *Apostles of the Boreal* was written and/or workshopped, and produced as a chapbook, for Mary Dalton's course in Advanced Creative Writing: Poetry, Memorial University.

The title of the poem "Ice Flows and Sound Retreats" derives from Jan Kabatoff's art installation of the same name (The Rooms Art Gallery, St. John's, 2009/10).

Finally, thanks to my children, Ella and Ezra, for always inspiring me and sharing the wonders and joys of our own craggy piece of paradise.

Photo credit: Sheilagh O'Leary

About the Author

Alison Dyer's poetry and short stories have been published in *The Fiddlehead*, *Riddle Fence*, *Grain*, *The Newfoundland Quarterly*, *Rhythm Poetry Magazine*, *The Feathertale Review*, *3 Elements Literary Review*, *The Nashwaak Review*, *Grimm Magazine*, the *Cuffer Anthology* and *WDRC's Phoenix Anthology*. Her writings have twice won the NL Arts & Letters Awards. Dyer has an M.Sc. in physical geography, grew up in England and Quebec, and now divides her time between St. John's and Hant's Harbour, Newfoundland.